Americans All biographies are inspiring life stories about people of all races, creeds, and nationalities who have uniquely contributed to the American way of life. Highlights from each person's story develop his contributions in his special field — whether they be in the arts, industry, human rights, education, science and medicine, or sports.

Specific abilities, character, and accomplishments are emphasized. Often despite great odds, these famous people have attained success in their fields through the good use of ability, determination, and hard work. These fast-moving stories of real people will show the way to better understanding of the ingredients necessary for personal success.

Knute Rockne

NOTRE DAME'S FOOTBALL GREAT

by George Sullivan

illustrated by Dom Lupo

GARRARD PUBLISHING COMPANY
CHAMPAIGN, ILLINOIS

Picture credits:

Bagby Photo Company, South Bend, Indiana: P. 2, 20-21, 40, 53
Brown Brothers: P. 76
United Press International: P. 58, 61
Wide World Photos: P. 71

Copyright © 1970 by George Sullivan

All rights reserved. Manufactured in the U.S.A.

Standard Book Number: 8116-4561-4

Library of Congress Catalog Card Number: 70-113837

Contents

1. From Norway to Notre Dame . . 7
2. College Hero 17
3. Rockne Takes Over 28
4. The Four Horsemen 49
5. Good Times and Bad 67
6. "A National Loss" 85

1. From Norway to Notre Dame

Young Knute Rockne's restless spirit got the best of him and he wandered away from his family. He became fascinated by a group of Indian boys in feathered headdresses who were having a fine time whooping it up. Five-year-old Knute could not resist joining in their fun.

The Rockne family was visiting the World's Columbian Exposition of 1893 in Chicago, the World's Fair of that day.

"Oh, where can that boy have gone?" sobbed Knute's mother, dabbing her eyes with a handkerchief.

"We'll find him. Don't worry," Knute's father assured her.

"Don't worry, ma'am," said a police officer. "He's got to be around here someplace."

The search continued. It was not long before an officer saw an astounding sight as he passed the Indian encampment. A swarm of youngsters was scampering about. All the boys had copper skin and jet-black hair except for one. The policeman snatched off the boy's headdress —there was blond-haired, fair-skinned Knute Rockne.

Mrs. Rockne, young Knute, and his two sisters, Anna and Martha, had recently arrived in Chicago from their native Norway. Mrs. Rockne, who was usually very watchful of her brood, had made the trip without a single problem except those created by adventuresome Knute.

In New York, when Mrs. Rockne was preparing to leave the ship, Knute was missing. He was finally found in the crow's nest, the tiny shelter atop the towering mast.

Lars Rockne, Knute's father, had made the Atlantic crossing eighteen months before. Lars had come to America to exhibit a handsome two-wheeled carriage manufactured in the family business in Norway. The idea of exhibiting in America appealed to this venturesome Norseman. Besides, Lars knew of several families that had left Norway to settle in the United States. When they wrote back they described the country as the land of opportunity. "Our life could be better there," thought Lars.

Although his carriage won a medal at the fair, Lars received very few orders. He decided to settle in Chicago where he got a job as a machinist and went to school at night to study the English language.

When Mrs. Rockne and the children arrived, the family moved into a two-story brick house on the north side of the city. The neighborhood was known as the Logan Square district and was populated mostly by Irish and Swedish immigrants.

Knute was a healthy boy, sturdy and broad shouldered, but small for his age. He had a fine mind and an excellent memory. He entered Brentano Grammar School and began to bring home report cards that made his parents proud.

Young Knute got his first taste of American sports playing baseball and football on neighborhood corner lots. He made up for his lack of size by his ability to run fast.

Although the boys had no helmets,

shoulder pads, or other protective equipment, the football games were fierce and violent. One day Knute returned home with his clothes torn and an eye blackened.

"No more football for you," his father ordered. "From now on stick to baseball."

Knute had even worse luck on the diamond, however. He was accidentally struck across the face with a bat and his nose was flattened.

"You think football is rough," he said to his father. "I got this nose from baseball." Baseball then became the forbidden sport for Knute, and football was permitted again.

Knute entered Northwest Division High School (now Tuley High School) at the age of thirteen. He made the track team, specializing in the half-mile run. He also tried out for football, but his size was against him, and he did not make the varsity until his senior year.

During Knute's senior year in high school, the principal dissolved the school track team because the boys had skipped classes to practice. Knute was so upset he threatened to leave school and find a job.

The Rockne family was growing. Two more daughters, Louise and Florence, had been born. Knute's father could use another pay envelope and he did not try to persuade his son to remain in school. Knute left school and went to work.

He drifted from one job to another, then took a job as a clerk in the Chicago post office. There he toiled from midnight until 8:30 A.M. six days a week, handling mail sacks that weighed about fifty pounds each. It was rough, dirty work and paid only six hundred dollars a year.

Knute kept up his interest in sports,

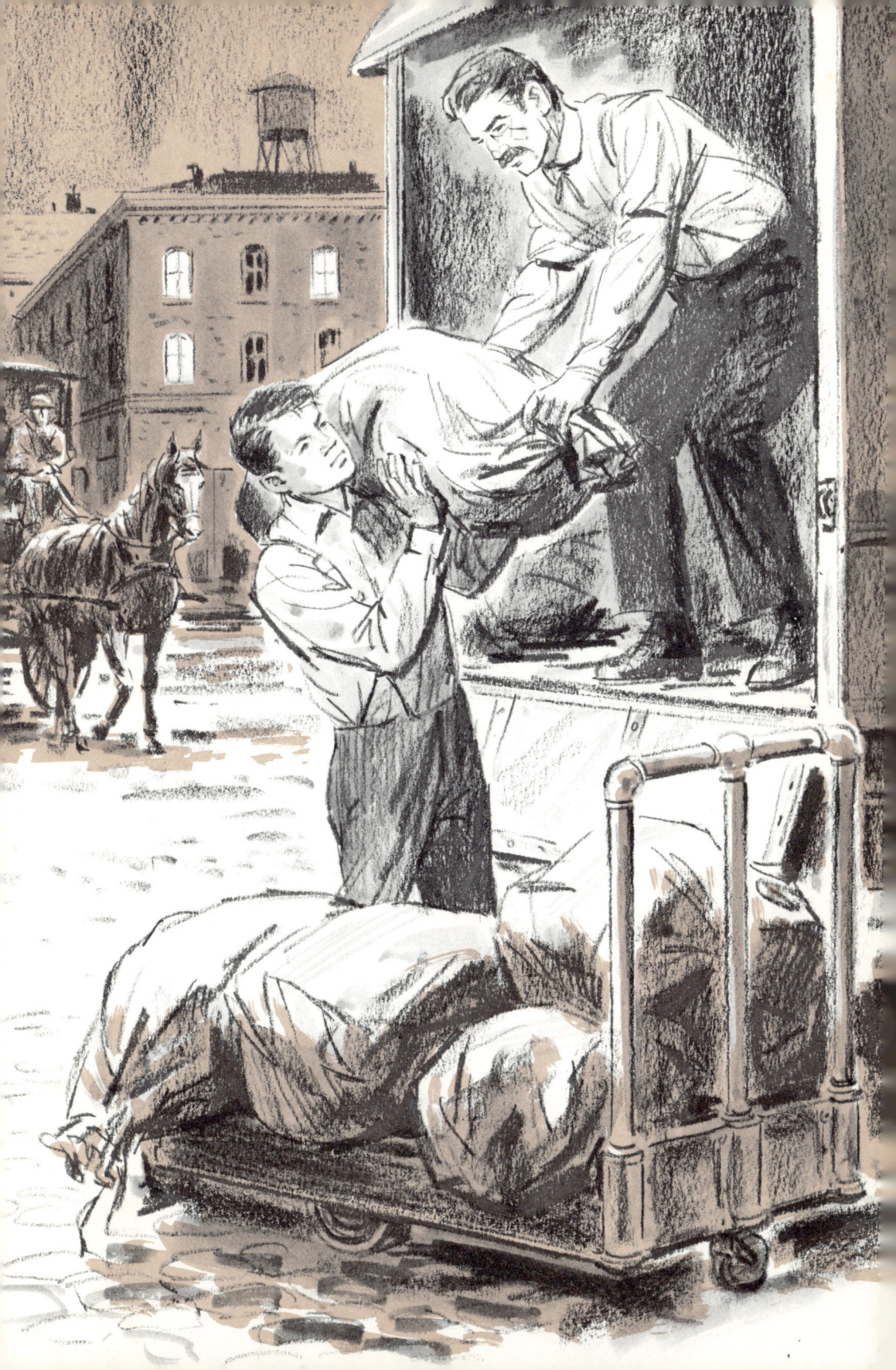

however, especially in track. He ran for the Irving Park Athletic Club, the Illinois Athletic Club, and the Central YMCA. He once won a half-mile race in two minutes and two seconds, which was considered good time in those days.

After he had been working at the post office for about a year, one of his sisters said to him, "Knute, you're wasting your time in this job. You should go on to college."

"I don't know," he answered. "I haven't done much studying since I left high school. I'm pretty rusty."

His sister persisted. "It would mean so much to the family," she said. "It would make us all proud of you. And now that we older girls are working, we're able to help out financially."

She also had one last argument. "You wouldn't have to give up sports," she pointed out. "You could be on the college track team."

His sister's encouragement kindled the flame of ambition in Knute. He began to study and save his money so that he could go to college. He set a thousand dollars as his goal.

He planned to attend the University of Illinois. When he revealed his intention to Johnny Devine and Johnny Plant, two of his friends, they were not enthusiastic about his choice.

"Why Illinois?" Plant asked. "Why don't you come with us? We're going to Notre Dame."

Rockne scoffed at the idea. "Notre Dame?" he said. "Who ever heard of Notre Dame? They never won a football game in their lives."

"You can get a job there," Devine said. "It will help you to pay your expenses."

Now Knute was listening carefully.

"It doesn't cost so much to go to Notre Dame either," Devine continued. "The tuition is much less than at Illinois."

Knute was won over. He would go to Notre Dame.

When he presented himself at the school, he was told he would have to take an entrance examination because he had no high school diploma. "The passing grade is high," the dean said. "It's eighty." Knute scored an eighty-seven.

Knute was thrilled by his success. Now the whole idea of going to college excited him.

2. College Hero

Knute was an extremely serious-minded student, perhaps because of his age. He was now twenty-two, four years older than the average freshman. Because of his misshapen nose, the result of his brush with the baseball bat, and because he was already beginning to grow bald, he looked even older.

Rockne's strongest subject was chemistry, and this was the reason he enrolled in the College of Pharmacy. A professor there later described him as the school's "best man in chemistry."

Rockne's favorite method of study was to place a book open flat on the desk in front of him. After reading a few paragraphs he would walk up and down, rolling a pencil between the palms of his hands and mulling over what he had just read. Anyone who interrupted him would be invited to discuss whatever Rockne was studying. In this way he helped to fix the subject in his memory.

Knute's grades were almost always in the 90's. Only in his junior year, when his father died, did his marks slip. He was graduated *summa cum laude*—"with highest praise."

To earn money to pay his expenses, Knute got a job as janitor in the science laboratory. He also waited on tables.

Then he learned that anyone who became a member of the college band would receive a reduction in tuition. So Rockne decided to join the band—as a flute player. He practiced endlessly in the dormitory, but one problem developed. Sometimes, in order to get some silence, his roommates would hide the evil instrument.

The stage attracted him and he joined the college drama group. He was such a skilled actor that he was given all the female roles. At various times he was an Indian squaw, a society matron, and a shopgirl.

Somehow Rockne also managed to find time for sports. During his sophomore year he won a starting spot on the football team as a fleet-footed end. For two consecutive years Notre Dame went undefeated, but its opponents were mostly small schools that were not widely known.

In the summer before their senior year, Rockne and Gus Dorais, the Notre Dame quarterback, obtained jobs as lifeguards

at Cedar Point, Ohio, a resort area on Lake Erie. They tucked a football into their luggage with the rest of their belongings.

Notre Dame was scheduled to play Army at West Point in the fall. Never before had the "Fighting Irish," as the Notre Dame team was called, faced such a noteworthy opponent as the team from the United States Military Academy. Rockne and Dorais knew it would be a glorious day

Notre Dame players Rockne (first row right) and Dorais (second row right) in 1913

if Notre Dame could whip the cadets.

The two boys worked out a plan they were sure would bring the Notre Dame team to victory. In those days football teams frowned on using the forward pass. They felt it was too complicated.

"If Army doesn't believe in the pass," Dorais said, "we'll practice it until we know it perfectly."

Rockne was quick to agree. "We'll give them a surprise they'll never forget," he said.

All summer long they practiced long hours on the white, sandy beach. They tried passes of all types—long passes and short ones, fast bullets and soft feathery tosses. Dorais became remarkably accurate with the ball, and Rockne learned to gather in everything his teammate threw.

Most receivers caught the ball with their arms and then clutched it to their chest. It was a clumsy method and they often fumbled. Rockne learned to grab the ball with his fingertips. He found he could make a catch without breaking stride, and he was far less likely to fumble.

Notre Dame met Army on November 1, 1913. The date shines brightly in Notre Dame football history, although only a few thousand people saw what happened.

The game was supposed to be only a light workout for the powerful Army team. "Why bother going?" most people figured. The first quarter went as everyone expected, with the much heavier Army team pushing Notre Dame all over the field. "It's time we opened up," said Dorais.

Dorais called the signals. The ball was snapped back. In rushed the huge Army guards and tackles. Dorais danced back, then deftly tossed the ball to Notre Dame right halfback, Joe Pliska, for an eleven-yard gain and a first down.

"Just an accident," said one Army player. Dorais did it again and again, using both Pliska and Rockne as his targets.

Now Dorais and Rockne unveiled a well-rehearsed piece of strategy. After a fierce pileup, Rockne emerged limping. On the next play he hobbled down the field. The defenseman covered him closely. On the next play Rockne did it again. This time the defender relaxed.

"O.K., Rock," said Dorais in the huddle, "this time it's coming to you."

Rockne started limping downfield. The defenseman practically yawned when he saw he was coming. Suddenly Rockne exploded, leaving the bewildered defenseman in the dust. Dorais let fire. The throw was perfect. Rockne's fingers closed around the ball at the goal line for a touchdown.

This was only the beginning. Before the baffled cadets knew what was happening, Notre Dame scored another touchdown. Now the score was 14–13.

Before the teams came out on the field for the third quarter, Army changed its strategy. The cadets' coach spread out the team's defenders to stop the passes.

Dorais was ready for such tactics. He abandoned the pass and turned to running plays. Time and time again his backs made long gains against the scattered Army defenders.

Then Dorais noticed that Army had closed up again to stop the runs. "Rock," he said in the huddle, "get set for a long one." Again the cadets were caught off guard. Indeed Army seemed helpless through most of the rest of the day. The final score saw Notre Dame on top, 35–13. Sports fans throughout the country were in a state of shock.

"Notre Dame?" said one. "I never heard of them."

"Where are they from?" asked another.

"Some little place in Indiana," came back the answer. "I think they call it South Bend."

The electrifying victory over Army was

an important turning point for Notre Dame and for Knute Rockne, too. Soon, the whole country would know of both.

While Rockne and Dorais worked as lifeguards at Cedar Point, Knute was attracted by a small, dark-haired girl named Bonnie Skiles. He had always been bashful and self-conscious around girls. Meeting one for the first time, he would blush to his hairline, but with Bonnie it was different. She made Knute feel comfortable and assured. As for Bonnie, she could not resist Knute's shy charm.

The records of Saints Peter and Paul Church in Sandusky, Ohio, indicate the happy ending. There, on July 15, 1914, Knute Kenneth Rockne was wed to Bonnie Gwendoline Skiles.

3. Rockne Takes Over

After they graduated both Rockne and Dorais decided to turn to coaching. They learned that Loras College in Dubuque, Iowa, was seeking a coach.

"Let's flip a coin to see which one of us applies for the job," Dorais said.

Rockne agreed. Dorais tossed a coin in the air.

"Call it," he said.

"Heads," Rockne declared.

It came up tails.

At first Rockne was disappointed by this turn of fate. Then Jesse Harper, the Notre

Dame football coach, came to Knute with an exciting proposal.

"Why not help me out as assistant football coach?" he said. "We also need a head track coach. You could handle that job, too."

Rockne needed no urging. He quickly decided to stay on at Notre Dame. In addition to carrying on his coaching duties, he became an instructor in chemistry. Now, with a wife to support, he could use the extra money.

As assistant to Jesse Harper, Rockne coached the linemen. He introduced them to a unique blocking style, one that was born out of his experience as a player.

Rockne, when playing end, often found himself pitted against men who outweighed him by fifty or sixty pounds. The system of blocking used in those days called for the blocker to drive straight ahead into the man he was blocking, but this wouldn't work for Rockne; he was too small.

Instead he learned to come at an opponent from a low crouch, his legs spread wide apart. To surprise the man he was blocking, Rockne always attacked from a different angle.

Rockne achieved considerable success with this blocking style. Eventually it led to the general use of single-man blocking, wherein one man blocked one man. Up

until Rockne's time teams used two-man blocking, that is, two men against one man.

One day Rockne explained to the squad his theories on blocking. "Now let's see what you can do," he said.

In the practice session that followed, Rockne noticed that Joe Bachman, a veteran first-string player, was not following instructions. He took Bachman aside and demonstrated the new technique.

Practice resumed, and again Bachman ignored Rockne's suggestions.

"That's all for you, Bachman," Rockne bellowed. "Turn in your uniform. You're through!"

The rest of the squad was stunned. No assistant coach had ever fired a regular before.

Coach Harper had witnessed what had taken place. He walked over to Bachman.

"You heard what Coach Rockne said," Harper declared. "Turn in your uniform."

After practice was over Bachman went to see Harper. He promised he would follow Rockne's instructions. The next day Bachman apologized to Rockne in front of the entire squad. No player ever questioned Rockne's authority again.

In 1914, Rockne's first year as an assistant coach, Notre Dame had a fine team. The team's schedule called for it to play Yale University in New Haven. The Irish were confident, but Yale, using new and clever plays, completely bewildered them, whipping Notre Dame by a score of 28–0. Harper and Rockne were upset by the defeat. They had long discussions on how they might improve the team.

"We've got to make some changes," Harper declared. "Suppose we start shifting the backs."

Rockne was familiar with the shift. A few colleges had been experimenting with it. Just before the ball was centered, each backfield man took a step to the right or left, following a signal given by the quarterback. Before the defense could adjust to the new formation, the play was run off.

A gleam came into Rockne's eye. "Let's do it," he urged. "The other team will never know where we're going to strike."

Then Rockne suggested a new wrinkle. "Let's shift the ends along with the backs."

Harper liked the idea. "That'll make it even more baffling," he said.

The Notre Dame shift was immediately popular with both players and fans. It relied upon speed and timing and stressed brains, not brawn.

Before the 1918 season opened, Jesse Harper resigned. He recommended to the university officials that Rockne be named to succeed him.

"But he's too young," said one official. "He's only twenty-nine."

"Forget his age," Harper answered. "He's intelligent and loyal. He has an electric personality and handles players better than anyone I know."

"Besides," Harper continued, "I've already promised him the job."

"Well, if you've made him a promise, we have no choice but to honor it," said the official. "We'll give him a chance."

Rockne was thrilled with his new assignment. He looked upon the increased responsibility as an exciting challenge. The additional salary he was to receive was also important to him, for his family was growing. There were now two sons.

Billy, the Rocknes' first boy, was born in 1915. With Billy's arrival Rockne pitched in with the household chores to help the new mother. He even prepared meals. His one specialty was ham and eggs. When he invited friends to his home for dinner, he'd sometimes tell them, "And I'll cook the meal myself."

The guests knew what to expect on the menu. "Don't tell us," they would joke, "that you've found a new way to cook ham and eggs?"

The second son, Knute, Jr., was born to the Rocknes in 1918. In spite of the long hours Rockne devoted to coaching, he did not neglect his children. In the backyard or on the beach, he tossed a football to his sons. He tried out jokes on the boys while giving them their baths.

Rockne wanted his sons to become interested in football, but he never forced the game upon them. He did, however, leave footballs around the house and have uniforms made for the two boys.

When the children grew old enough to travel, he sometimes took them on football trips with him. Billy, the older son, was a familiar figure on the Notre Dame practice field during his grade-school years.

When Rockne took over as head coach, Notre Dame football was a far cry from what it is today. He had no staff, and besides his coaching duties he had to struggle to find opponents to fill out the team's schedule. He also served as chief ticket seller, business manager, and publicity man. Games were played on the campus at Cartier Field. The rickety stands could hold only twenty-five hundred people. Other college stadiums held fifty thousand people.

During 1918, Rockne's first season, the country was recovering from World War I. Notre Dame, like most other colleges, played a shortened schedule. The team won three games, lost one, and tied two.

The next year, when colleges began playing normal schedules, Rockne had ready a secret weapon. The name of his weapon was George Gipp (pronounced with a hard *G* as in gift). Tall and trim, Gipp was an athlete of exceptional skills.

His specialty was dropkicking, a football art that has since been discarded in favor of the place kick. In the dropkick the player dropped the ball to the ground nose first, then kicked it just as it started to rebound. The play was used to score field goals or points after a touchdown.

In 1919, Gipp's junior year, Notre Dame met a high-powered Army team. The cadets rolled to a 9-0 lead. The contest came in the closing seconds of the first half. The Irish had the ball on Army's one-yard line. Did Notre Dame have enough time to run another play?

At that time there was no scoreboard clock as there is today. The referee kept the time. Gipp saw the referee look at his watch, and begin to raise his hand to signal the end of the half.

"Quick, give me the ball!" Gipp yelled at the center. "Hurry!"

Snatching the ball Gipp dove over the goal line. At the same instant, the gun went off, ending the half. Because the ball was in play before the gun sounded, the touchdown counted.

The Irish were fired up by Gipp's shrewdness. They held Army scoreless in the second half and put the winning touchdown across late in the game.

Notre Dame did not lose a single game during the 1919 season. Yet Rockne's

Coach Rockne and his Fighting Irish at a practice session in the early 1920's

success was not just a matter of football victories. This is what the sports editor of *The Dome*, the Notre Dame school paper, was to say about Rockne:

> Rockne loves his boys and he labors to turn them out as men. He believes that athletics are a valuable preparation for future life, and his theory is that physical contact gives the athlete the moral confidence to "go out and crack 'em" after the school days are over.
>
> He is strong, courageous and determined; he is also lovable, delightful and witty. He is stern but considerate. The whole school is behind Rock.

Gipp was Rockne's big gun in 1920.

That season he put on a spectacular one-man show against Army. He passed, punted, and drop-kicked. In the open field he was as unstoppable as falling water. The Irish won, 27-17, their fifth straight triumph of the season.

Gipp was a man of tremendous courage. In the early stages of the game against Indiana that season, he injured his shoulder. Teams did not have doctors on the bench in those days to diagnose injuries. All Gipp knew was that he was in intense pain. Rockne kept him on the bench.

The Indiana players, sensing that they might be able to upset the Irish with Gipp on the sidelines, forged to a 10-7 lead. In the final minutes of the game, the man who had replaced Gipp was injured.

Rockne turned to George. "Can you go back in?" he asked. Gipp's face broke into a smile. "Sure," he said, and without a second's hesitation he grabbed his helmet and sprinted out onto the field.

Notre Dame had the ball on the Indiana five-yard line. Gipp carried, slamming into the Indiana line. It held, with no gain for Notre Dame. Gipp took the ball again. This time he battered his way into the end zone. The final score read: Notre Dame 13; Indiana, 10.

George Gipp had saved the day—with a broken collarbone.

The next week Gipp was in uniform when the team played Northwestern, but his injured shoulder was heavily padded with bandaging. Even without the Gipper in the line-up, Notre Dame cruised to a 26–0 lead.

Late in the game a loud chant began to rise from the packed stadium.

"Gipp . . . Gipp . . . Gipp."

The contest had been decided, but the

crowd wanted to see Notre Dame's splendid hero.

"They're crazy," thought Rockne. "How can I put an injured boy into the game?"

The chant became a roar.

"Gipp . . . Gipp . . . We want Gipp!"

Suddenly Rockne was struck with a wild idea. He would satisfy the crowd. He would put Gipp in, but as a defensive man. Gipp would thus be able to avoid contact.

The crowd let out a tremendous roar when Gipp ran out onto the field. The ball was punted toward him. He let it roll dead.

Now Notre Dame took over. On the first play Gipp merely kept out of the way to avoid getting mauled. On the next play, however, Gipp got the ball and drifted back to pass. Rockne watched, wide-eyed and open-mouthed.

Gipp fired, throwing the ball with wrist action, without moving his shoulder. Norm Barry, the Notre Dame receiver, grabbed the ball and galloped for a touchdown.

When Gipp came off the field, Rockne rushed out to meet him. He waggled his finger in the young man's face. "What if you had been hurt?" he said. "What would people have said about my letting you into the game with a broken collarbone?" George just grinned.

The following week Notre Dame overwhelmed Michigan A&M, and with this victory completed its second consecutive undefeated season. As for Gipp, he was named an All-American, the first Notre Dame player to receive this recognition.

About two weeks after the season ended, Gipp was stricken with a sore throat that led to pneumonia. He was taken to the hospital, where his condition grew worse.

Then it became known: George Gipp was dying. Penicillin, which might have cured his illness, had not yet been discovered.

Rockne was among the small cluster of grief-stricken friends who visited Gipp in the quiet hospital room. Gipp lay still. He was deathly white. "It's tough," someone whispered.

Gipp heard. "What's tough about it?" he said. "I've got to go. I'm not afraid."

Then Gipp turned his face to Rockne and made a request. "Rock," he said, "someday when the team is finding the going rough, when the boys are getting beaten, tell them to fight back with all they've got. Tell them to win one for the Gipper."

Tears welled up in Rockne's eyes, but he nodded quietly, reaching out a hand to grasp one of Gipp's hands in his own.

A few days later the young hero died. All business stopped in South Bend. Fifteen hundred Notre Dame students escorted the casket to the railroad station. The football team walked as a unit, with the position of left halfback vacant. A train waited to carry the body to Gipp's home in Michigan for burial.

The drama and tragedy of Gipp's death was front-page news across the country. Statements of praise for the young athlete poured forth. Of all that was said and written about him, Gipp himself probably would have liked Rockne's tribute best. Years later, writing for a national magazine, Rockne declared: "George Gipp was the greatest football player Notre Dame ever produced."

4. The Four Horsemen

Because he was small, Rockne, as a player, had to rely on speed and intelligence to outdo big and brawny opponents. As a coach he taught his football teams the value of mental ability. He once said: "Before you can defeat your opponent, you've got to outthink him."

The backfield shift and one-on-one blocking are examples of Rockne's use of brainpower to overcome enemy teams. Late in 1922 he introduced another piece of football magic.

In a game that season against Butler University, an Indianapolis school, Paul Castner, Notre Dame's star fullback, was injured. To the surprise of the experts, Rockne replaced Castner with a lightweight speedster named Elmer Layden, a one-time track star.

Traditionally the fullback had always been a heavy, battering-ram type of player. Layden, as Rockne described him, was a "saber instead of a club." Layden's great speed enabled him to pierce enemy defenses, even though each man in the opposing line outweighed him by twenty pounds and more.

Layden was the final building stone in a backfield that was to become the most famous in all football history—the Four Horsemen. For three seasons the Four

Horsemen rode roughshod over virtually every team Notre Dame faced.

Actually the Four Horsemen were only pony-sized. Layden weighed 168 pounds; quarterback Harry Stuhldreher, 154, and halfbacks Don Miller and Jim Crowley, 165 pounds each. Each man was as elusive as a cake of soap in the bathtub. Speed was their chief weapon.

Rockne's cleverness made them even faster. In practice sessions he had each man wear extra-heavy equipment. On the day of the game, they donned equipment of normal weight. They felt faster—and they were.

The quartet was first dubbed "the Four Horsemen" one October afternoon in 1924 when Notre Dame trimmed Army at the packed Polo Grounds in New York City.

Grantland Rice, the most noted sportswriter of the day, covered the game. He wrote one of the most famous sports stories of all time. It began:

Polo Grounds, New York, Oct. 19, 1924—Outlined against a blue-gray October sky, the Four Horsemen rode again. In dramatic lore they are known as Famine, Pestilence, Destruction, and Death. These are only aliases. Their real names are Stuhldreher, Miller, Crowley, and Layden. They formed the crest of the South Bend cyclone before which another fighting Army football team was swept over the precipice of the Polo Grounds yesterday afternoon....

Rice's story might have been forgotten except for a shrewd young man named

George Strickler who served as Notre Dame's publicity man. The Monday following the Army game, Strickler hired four horses from a riding stable and brought them to the practice field.

Rockne could hardly believe his eyes when he saw the horses being led toward him. The players stopped their practice to watch. Rockne fumed.

Notre Dame's celebrated "Four Horsemen"

"Get those horses out of here," he shouted. "We're trying to practice."

Strickler explained the valuable publicity to be gained from publicizing "the Four Horsemen." Reluctantly Rockne yielded to the persuasive young man.

Stuhldreher, Crowley, Miller, and Layden had their picture taken astride the horses. The picture was printed in almost every newspaper in the country. The term "Four Horsemen" became forever locked with Notre Dame in the minds of sports fans everywhere. The Four Horsemen lost only two games in three years. Rockne hated to lose, but when a rare loss did befall the team, he accepted it.

During the 1922 season, unbeaten Notre Dame faced unbeaten Nebraska in the final game of the season. The Nebraskans were big and tough. In the first half they built a 14–0 lead.

The Notre Dame players came out fighting in the second half. They scored one touchdown in the third quarter and, as the game entered its final minutes, they were battling for another.

Harry Stuhldreher went back to pass. He spotted his receiver. He cocked his arm. Suddenly a 250-pound Nebraska tackle crashed through the line and thumped the 154-pound Stuhldreher to the ground before he could release the ball. So ended Notre Dame's scoring threat. Nebraska won, 14–6.

That night Rockne went to the players' hotel rooms. He congratulated each boy. "You gave everything you had," he said. "You've never played, nor will you ever play, a game of which you can feel more proud."

Victory, since it was achieved so often, was more of a problem than defeat.

Rockne was careful not to let the Four Horsemen get too high an opinion of themselves. He made them realize that their success was the result of a team effort—their own talents *plus* those of the seven linemen. To make this clear, Rockne in practice sessions sometimes used the Four Horsemen backfield behind a line made up of second-string players.

Stuhldreher would then call a play. Immediately the opposing team would break through to dump the runner or bat down the pass.

"What's the matter with you fellows?" Rockne would ask. "Can't you get anyplace?"

Then he'd put in the first-string linemen. "Now let's see you go," he'd say.

Rockne indeed knew human psychology. Often he used this knowledge to get the most out of the team.

During the 1925 season Notre Dame played Northwestern University at South Bend. The Irish players were listless during the first half, and Northwestern built a 10–0 lead. In the locker room at half time, the players waited nervously for Rockne to appear. They knew they were in for a tongue-lashing. They waited and waited. Where was Rockne?

Suddenly the coach burst into the room. He was boiling. "So you call yourselves the Fighting Irish?" he began. "You look like a bunch of peaceful Swedes to me.

"It looks like Notre Dame is about to lose its first home game in twenty years. Just think, some day you'll be able to tell your children and grandchildren how you once had the 'honor' of disgracing Notre Dame."

He glared at his men. The locker room became as silent as a tomb.

Rockne taught his players the value of team effort as well as new football plays.

Then Rockne turned to his assistant coach, Heartly (Hunk) Anderson, and said in a loud voice, "From now on, Hunk, they're all yours. I'm through with them." With that he strode from the room.

The players almost broke the door down in their haste to get out onto the field to redeem themselves. They played smart, hard-hitting football, marching to one touchdown and then another. When the game ended, the scoreboard read: Notre Dame, 13; Northwestern, 10.

Rockne, of course, had no intention of leaving the team for good. Once he saw his men begin to play the type of football of which they were capable, he took his place on the bench.

While Rockne was often demanding and a stern disciplinarian on the football field, he was inclined to be easygoing in his own home.

One day Billy came into the house covered with mud. Rockne pretended he was angry. "How old are you?" he asked.

"I'm seven," the boy replied.

"I don't believe it," Rockne said. "No boy could get *that* dirty in only seven years."

A girl, Mary Jean, was born to the Rocknes in 1920. Rockne had a playful way of dealing with her. Once he told Mary Jean that her birthday present was to be "something for your neck." The girl thought she might receive a necklace or a scarf.

One day not long after, she came running into the house, completely grimy from scuffling with her brothers.

Rockne looked at her, a twinkle in his eye. "Now I'm going to give you your birthday present," he said. "It's a bar of soap."

Always a coach, Rockne gives his small son some tips on hitting a golf ball.

Rockne found that one of the drawbacks of being Notre Dame's coach was the fact that he had to be away from his wife and children for long periods of time. Even when Rockne traveled, however, his family never left his thoughts. He never failed to telephone when he reached a distant city, and once, he began a radio interview with the words, "Hello, Bonnie and the children."

Led by the Four Horsemen, Notre Dame rolled to an undefeated, untied season in 1924. Then Rockne was invited to bring the team to the Rose Bowl in Pasadena, California, to meet Stanford University, the West Coast champion. In those days the Rose Bowl game decided the national championship among college teams.

Rockne knew that the Eastern team in the Rose Bowl was always handicapped by the change in climate. Players who were used to frigid winter temperatures often wilted in the extreme heat of that part of California.

Rockne had a plan to solve this problem. The team's first Rose Bowl practice was scheduled at 3:00 P.M. on the Friday before the game. When the players boarded the bus to take them to the stadium, Rockne made an announcement. "I know many of you boys have never been on the West Coast," he said, "so before we head for the Rose Bowl we're going to do a little sightseeing."

The news delighted the players. Rockne turned to the driver of the bus. "Just follow me," he said. Then Rockne got into his automobile to lead the way.

They covered Los Angeles from one end to the other. Three o'clock passed, then four. The players began to grow anxious. They kept looking at their watches.

"Hey, driver," one player called out. "When do we head for practice?"

"My orders are to follow Coach Rockne," the driver said. "That's all I know."

It was six o'clock when Rockne pulled up to the Rose Bowl. The players donned their uniforms and went out onto the field. The shadows of early evening had melted the day's intense heat. It was agreeably cool.

"Where's all that hot weather we've been hearing about?" said one player.

"Yeah," another said, "this is great."

Rockne turned to one of his assistant coaches. "Well, I guess it worked," he said. "First impressions are the ones that last. Even if it's a hundred and ten degrees on the day of the game, I doubt they'll notice it."

The game was a thriller. Stanford scored first on a field goal, but Notre Dame charged back with a touchdown to give the Irish a 6–3 lead.

In the second quarter Elmer Layden intercepted a pass on the Notre Dame 15-yard line and flashed 85 yards for a touchdown. That made the score 13–3 in favor of Notre Dame.

The Irish scored again in the third

quarter, boosting their lead to 20–3, but the game still was not safe. Stanford's All-American fullback, big Ernie Nevers, ripped wide holes in the Irish line. Stanford scored its first touchdown and then threatened another, rampaging to a first down on the Notre Dame two-yard line.

The stage was set for a glittering moment in Notre Dame football history. Nevers hurled his bulk into the Notre Dame line. He gained a foot. He tried again. Another foot, no more. Nevers tried a third time. He got about a yard. One more chance for Stanford to make an advance remained.

Rockne sent a substitute tackle, John McMullen, into the game. The team crowded around McMullen for words of advice and inspiration from the bench.

"What did Rock say?" asked several players, all talking at once.

The coach's instructions were simple. "Rock said to hold 'em," McMullen answered.

The team did exactly that. Nevers slammed into the middle again. The line was a stone wall. The Irish stopped the Stanford fullback inches short of the goal.

Layden punted out of trouble. Stanford took over and hammered toward the Irish end zone again. The Stanford quarterback called a sideline pass. He threw. Layden, turning on his lightning speed, intercepted and rocketed away on a 60-yard touchdown run. Jim Crowley booted the extra point. Notre Dame led, 27–10. Minutes later the final gun sounded. The Four Horsemen had achieved their greatest triumph.

5. Good Times and Bad

In his first year as Notre Dame's head coach, Rockne attended a dinner at which he was called upon to speak. He found his hands quivering as he took the microphone. He stuttered and stammered so much he could hardly make himself understood. He felt ashamed and he made up his mind to overcome this failing. He sought advice from Father John W. Cavanagh, president of the university, and a noted public speaker.

"I have no trouble talking to football players or students in my chemistry classes," Rockne explained. "But when I get up before a mixed group, I get flustered."

Father Cavanagh gave Rock this advice: "Study your audience and concentrate on what will appeal to the majority. Plan a beginning and an end. Be brief.

"And remember," the priest continued, "you have one thing few speakers have. You have a sense of humor. Use your wit in your speeches." Rockne followed this advice and eventually became one of the most famous after-dinner speakers in the country.

Besides his wit Rockne had a phenomenal memory that added to his skill as a speechmaker. His talks were filled with references to conversations he had heard or interesting facts he had read.

Reading was one of his greatest pleasures. He never failed to take up a book at night after the children had gone to bed. He read both for enjoyment and to educate himself.

He always had three books lined up on his night table—a detective novel, a volume of classical literature, and a scientific text. He would begin one, then, after a certain number of pages, turn to another. This habit of switching back and forth helped Rockne to develop his amazing memory.

Rockne seldom forgot a face. When he traveled with the team and people clustered about him, he would pick out a face in the crowd, then go over and shake the man's hand.

"It's Smith," he would say, "Bill Smith. I remember you from Milwaukee. How are you, Bill?"

Bill Smith would become a Rockne fan forever.

Rockne's winning personality made it necessary to use as many as twenty special trains any time Notre Dame traveled to Los Angeles to play Southern California. The trains were filled mostly with Rockne's friends and admirers.

To his players Rockne was much more than a coach. He was also a counselor and cherished friend. During the school year Rockne often invited groups of players to his home. On the practice field Rockne was a teacher and a trainer. In the classroom he was an instructor. In his home, amidst his family, however, he could be a fatherly adviser to his men.

When students gathered at the Rockne home, football was naturally the topic of conversation. Mrs. Rockne once said that she always knew when a group of boys had been at their home because the tables and chairs were left lined up to represent players in football formation.

Rockne continued to be a friend and adviser to his players after they were graduated. He liked to have them bring their problems to him. He was disappointed when they did not. One Notre

On the drill field and off, Coach Rockne had a lasting influence on his men.

Dame student graduate recalled, "I never made an important decision without Rockne's advice."

Rockne did not like to see his men enter professional football, a sport then in its infancy.

"They pay you enough for a few months' work, then there's nothing for you to do until the next season," he said. "You wind up without any profession, without any career."

Rockne advised his players to become college coaches instead. He took pleasure in helping them find coaching jobs, and they were not hard to find. Indeed so many colleges wanted Rockne graduates that Rockne had a waiting list of jobs.

Not every year was a winning year for Rockne. In 1928 Notre Dame won five games and lost four. Yet in one game that season, the spirit of the Fighting

Irish was set burning, and it blazed with dazzling brilliance.

The Irish traveled to New York City to play Army at Yankee Stadium. Undefeated Army was having one of its finest years. The cadets expected to add Notre Dame to their list of victims.

Surprisingly Notre Dame held Army even throughout the first half, but when the team filed into the locker room at half time, the men were battered and dog-weary. Powerful Army would surely crush the Irish in the second half.

Rockne looked at his bedraggled boys. Then he began to speak, his voice soft and low.

"Boys," he said, "I want to tell you the story of George Gipp."

Then Rockne poured out a gripping story, telling of Gipp's great skills, his daring exploits, and his tragic death.

"As Gipp lay dying," Rockne continued, "he turned to me and said, 'Rock, someday when the team is finding the going rough, when the boys are getting beaten, tell them to fight back with all they've got. Tell them to win one for the Gipper.'"

Rockne paused. Many years had passed since the death of George Gipp, but thoughts of him still brought tears to Rockne's eyes.

"Boys," he said, his voice growing louder and stronger, "this is that game." Now Rockne was on his feet. His words were a rallying cry. "This is the game to win for the Gipper!"

No team could have stopped the Irish that day. Late in the game the score was tied, 6–6. Notre Dame was on the march. The stands were in a frenzy, one roar blending with the next.

Niemiec, left, is about to throw the long pass which brought victory to Notre Dame.

Rockne sent two sophomore players into the game, Frank Carideo at quarterback, and Johnny O'Brien at end. Carideo called a reverse pass. The ball went to Johnny Niemiec. He dropped back to throw. Tacklers swarmed in on him.

O'Brien was sprinting downfield. At the last second Niemiec fired. The ball was a trifle high. O'Brien, running at top speed, juggled the ball. He was still juggling it when he fell over the goal line for the touchdown that put Notre Dame ahead, 12–6.

Seconds later the game ended. George Gipp had defeated Army.

Much of the rest of the season was filled with gloom, however. Rockne saw his team beaten at home for the first time in twenty-five years. For the first time in his coaching career, he saw his men lose two consecutive games.

Rockne used the 1928 season wisely, however, giving young sophomore players valuable game experience. He was sowing the seeds for future success.

Notre Dame opened the 1929 season by beating Indiana. After the game Rockne became ill and had to go to bed. Tom Lieb, the Notre Dame line coach, visited him. Rockne was reading a medical book.

"Tom," said Rockne sadly, "I believe I have phlebitis."

His diagnosis was correct. Phlebitis, a disease that causes inflammation of the veins, had affected his legs, causing him agonizing pain. Doctors ordered him to remain in bed.

As Rockne's trusted lieutenant, Tom Lieb directed the team. Before each game Rockne placed a telephone call to the team, giving advice and encouragement to each player.

The system worked well. Notre Dame roared to three straight victories without a loss. Tough Carnegie Tech was next. The game was to be played in Pittsburgh.

Tech had beaten the Irish in 1926 and 1928. The Tech men bragged that they were Notre Dame's "jinx team." Rockne was determined to stop such talk.

In the week before the game, he

watched the team's practice sessions from a wheelchair. A microphone and a loudspeaker were set up, and Rockne's voice boomed out instructions.

His doctors warned Rockne not to make the trip East with the team. "The excitement of the game could release a blood clot from your leg," one doctor explained, "and send it racing through your bloodstream and into your heart or brain. If this happens you might not return from Pittsburgh alive."

But when the train carrying the team left South Bend, Rockne was aboard. "He values winning more than living," wrote one newspaperman.

On the day of the game, Pitt Stadium was filled to overflowing long before game time. In the Notre Dame dressing room, one question was on everyone's lips: "Would Rockne be there?"

Suddenly the door opened. Tom Lieb entered, carrying Rockne in his arms. He placed him on a table. Rockne sat quietly, his face grim. He seemed barely aware that anyone else was present. Minutes before the team took the field, Rockne began to speak. His voice was confident.

"I don't know when I've ever wanted a game so much," he declared.

"This team is going to be tough. They think they have your number."

Then he paused. When he spoke again the words exploded.

"Why do you think I'm taking a chance like this? To see you lose?

"Go out there and crack 'em," he commanded. "Fight to win—WIN—WIN!"

Rockne watched the game from a wheelchair on the sidelines. The first half was scoreless. Notre Dame, a bit tense, fumbled the ball at crucial times.

At half time Rockne sought to relax his boys. He was as calm as an oyster in an ocean pool. "They're going to start passing," he said coolly. "Keep alert."

Notre Dame scored the game's first touchdown in the third quarter, then held off its tormentors the rest of the way. The final count was 7–0. The Tech jinx had been toppled.

With Carnegie Tech out of the way, the Irish handled Georgia Tech and Drake with comparative ease. The following week they took a thrill-packed game from Southern California, 13–12. Northwestern fell the next week, 26–0. Now only Army stood between Notre Dame and another unbeaten season.

The 1929 Army game was played in New York City on a frigid November day. The temperature stood at eight degrees above zero. The gridiron at Yankee

Stadium was frozen concrete-hard. Neither team could launch a scoring drive. It began to look as if the first team to get a touchdown would win.

Army had the ball on Notre Dame's 11-yard line. During the week Army had rehearsed a bold touchdown play to be used in such a situation. Now the Army team put it into use.

Chris Cagle, Army's always dangerous pass-or-run halfback, got the ball. He sprinted toward the left sideline, then stopped abruptly, turned, and fired a pass across the field to his right end.

It *was* a touchdown play—for Notre Dame.

Jack Elder, a Notre Dame defensive back, was sitting back and waiting. Timing his move perfectly Elder darted in front of the intended Army receiver and plucked the ball out of the arctic air.

Elder was a track star and he took off as if a starter's pistol had sounded, keeping close to the right sideline. An Army tackler made a flying leap for him at midfield—and missed. No one was close to Elder when he crossed into Army's end zone to score the game's only touchdown.

The Fighting Irish had achieved another unbeaten, untied season. Knute Rockne was riding high again.

6. "A National Loss"

It was 1930. Rockne was beginning his finest season—and his last.

He was as happy as he had ever been in his life. Graduation had been kind to the team. Almost every player on the 1929 squad would be returning. The phlebitis had subsided. He still had to wear rubber bandages on his legs, but his old enthusiasm and bounce had returned.

During the period of his illness, Rockne's main source of comfort had been Bonnie and the children. A fourth child and third son, John Vincent, nicknamed Jackie, had been born to the Rocknes in 1926.

Like the other boys in the family, Jackie was introduced to football at an early age. Once, when he was only four, he was practicing in the house and booted a football into a crystal chandelier, shattering it into countless fragments. Rockne did not scold or punish Jackie. Instead, the proud father complimented the boy on his kicking ability.

While his family was Rockne's chief source of happiness, Notre Dame's new stadium also gladdened his heart. It had been Rockne's dream for years, and he had supervised every detail of its construction. The stadium could seat fifty-eight thousand spectators. It was one of the most magnificent football showplaces in the nation.

Many people felt it should be named Rockne Stadium. To anyone who suggested that name to the man himself, Rockne gave a one-word answer: "No!"

Notre Dame Stadium was dedicated early in the 1930 season on a day when Notre Dame played Navy. The Irish were in good form, winning 26–2. Afterward, Bill Ingram, the Navy coach, said his team had faced the "greatest Notre Dame team in the history of football." Ingram was to prove a prophet.

The following week Notre Dame humbled Carnegie Tech, 20–6. Then the Notre Dame steamroller, gathering 35 points in the first half, flattened Pitt, 35–19.

Rockne used his second- and third-string players in the second half. "Thanks for being so kind to us," Pitt coach Jock Sutherland said after the game. "You could have scored a hundred points."

The Irish whipped Indiana the following week, and then traveled to Philadelphia for a game with Penn, the only Eastern appearance of the year for the Irish. The team was as perfect as any team can be. Before the first half ended, the Irish led, 43–0, and the final score was 60–20.

Drake, Northwestern, and Army fell in quick succession. Southern California was the one remaining opponent. The game was to be played in Los Angeles.

"They always expect me to pull a rabbit out of my hat when we come out here," Rockne said to a friend before the game, but the magician from South Bend was never in better form.

In the game against Southern California the previous year, Bucky O'Connor, a second-string halfback for the Irish, had been dealt a black eye. Rockne never let him forget the injury. Two days before the 1930 game against Southern California, Rockne made O'Connor a first-string halfback.

Early in the game the Irish had the ball on their own 20-yard line. O'Connor took the snap from center. A gaping hole suddenly opened on the right side of the Southern California line, and O'Connor waltzed through.

For a moment O'Connor seemed cut off at the sideline, but he gave the would-be tackler a change of pace and a quick sidestep, then broke into the open. The huge crowd was on its feet immediately and screaming.

"He's going all the way!" a fan shouted.

Blockers seemed to appear out of nowhere to clear O'Connor's path. He did not slow down until he reached Southern California's goal line.

Throughout the game O'Connor continued to stun the Trojans with his grace and speed. The young man scored two touchdowns and gained more yardage than the entire Southern California team. The game was a rout, Notre Dame winning, 27–0. The Irish had their second consecutive unbeaten season.

At the festive victory dinner for the team after the Southern California game, Rockne, his eyes sparkling, was strangely quiet. He appeared wholly contented; he seemed fulfilled.

Indeed he had a right to feel that way. In thirteen years as Notre Dame's coach, Rockne's teams had carved out an incredible record. They had played 122 games and had won 105. They had been beaten only twelve times. Five games had ended in ties.

No one knew it at the time, but the

victory over Southern California was the last game Rockne would ever coach.

In the spring of 1931 Rockne set out for the West Coast to deliver a speech in Los Angeles and attend meetings in Hollywood about a motion picture to be titled, *The Spirit of Notre Dame*. He boarded a train in Chicago bound for Kansas City. His two older sons, Bill and Knute, Jr., attended Pembroke Country Day School there, and Rockne planned a brief reunion with them. Rockne's train was late, however, and he had to go on without seeing the boys.

At 9:15 A.M. on March 31, 1931, Rockne climbed aboard the silver, three-engined Fokker airplane that was to take him to Los Angeles. The sky was overcast when the plane lumbered down the runway and clattered into the sky.

The fog grew dense, and soon the ship was swallowed up in it. The pilot was uncertain what to do—should he return to Kansas City or press on to Wichita farther west?

Commercial aviation was in its infancy in those days. Navigational instruments were primitive compared to the ones we have now. The pilot nosed his ship groundward hoping to catch sight of a familiar landmark. He watched the altimeter needle fall—1,200 feet . . . 1,000 . . . 750 . . . 500. Suddenly the side of a hill loomed up in front of him.

Local cattlemen on the ground heard what happened. First they heard the steady drone of the plane's engines, followed by a high-pitched roar as the ship fought for altitude. Then came the ear-splitting crash. Finally there was silence.

Besides Rockne the plane carried two pilots and five other passengers. There were no survivors. The Viking of football was dead.

"ROCKNE'S DEAD!" front-page headlines shouted across the nation.

An Atlanta newsboy read the headline and rubbed his eyes in disbelief. The Southern California band was giving a concert on the steps of the Oakland City

Hall when the news came. Immediately, they played taps.

When the news was received at Notre Dame, there were tears of unashamed grief. At once the school was closed. Teachers were not capable of teaching; students could not learn. A steady stream of grieving students hurried to the university chapel to offer prayers.

Messages of sympathy came from all over the country. President Herbert Hoover telegraphed to Mrs. Rockne: "Mr. Rockne so contributed to a cleanness and high purpose and sportsmanship in athletics that his passing is a national loss."

Rockne's grave in Highland Cemetery in South Bend is marked by a small headstone and is hard to find. But the monuments to the man are great and lasting. There is the huge stadium, which Rockne planned down to the brick and mortar.

There is the Knute Rockne Memorial Fieldhouse on the Notre Dame campus, erected by his friends.

Behind him as a living monument, Rockne also left coaches he had trained. They flooded the coaching ranks in the nation's high schools and colleges and in professional football for decades after Rockne's death.

The game of football itself is a monument to Rockne. Damon Runyon, the noted American journalist, wrote, "It was Rockne, with his marvelous Notre Dame teams and through his powerful personality, who made football the national institution it is today."

Last, there is the honor and tradition of Notre Dame. Walk on the campus and this spirit creeps up on you. During Rockne's years of gridiron glory this feeling ran deep, and it lingers to this day.